Joy
Is In The
Now Place

The Audacity To Be Present

Rochelle R. Asberry

Stephanie

Much Love

& Joy!

Rochelle

1

ISBN: 1530609291

ISBN-13: 978-1530609291

2

Dedication and Gratitude

- To my Lord and Savior, Jesus Christ, who gives me the example to live and love well; and to His Glory in all things.
- In loving memory, to my great-grandfather, Davis, with our mutual entrepreneurial spirit and to my great-grandmother, Adline, who loved her family dearly.
- In precious memory of Grammie Ida, for her hard work, love for me and for letting me eat ice cream before dinner.
- In memory of my very loving parents: My mother, Bettie, who had a "never give up" attitude and my dad, Albert, who was an avid reader and taught me to do the same.
- To my brother, Daimeone, who is 13 years younger than me and is one of the most intelligent people I know.
- To my husband, Dwayne, whom I love to call my personal chef. Thank you for the wonderful meals, and helping create fun and loving times in our marriage. By God's Grace, when we work together, we can do great things.
- To my wonderful daughter, Dominique, who teaches me to love unconditionally, who has a great sense of humor, and who reminds me to slow down when I need it.
- To my Spiritual Support/Church Family: Phillips Temple, CME Church, Indianapolis, IN; Senior Pastor, Oliver DeWayne Walker; and my Spiritual Mentor and friend, Rev. Alfreida Black and the entire ministerial staff.
- To the rest of my encouraging family members, friends, colleagues and clients who keep me accountable and responsible in my journey.

Contents

Welcome

I want to thank you for your interest in "Joy is in the Now Place."

This book is a reminder about being present, where your life truly is, to experience more sustainable joy, authentic self-knowledge and truth.

You are embarking on a wonderful inspirational journey. Living in our fast-paced world, imagine if you could pump your breaks, and slow down enough to gain more clarity, creativity and answers to your life. Would this be important to you? Well…in this book, you will find suggestions to help you overcome barriers and inspiration to live your best life. Each chapter is filled with practical tools, short stories, and blank sheets to give you an opportunity to jot down your thoughts and reflect.

Do not wait until someone gives you the green light. Give it to yourself. Do not sacrifice precious moments because you are wallowing in the past or floating around in the what ifs of the future. Allow yourself the audacity to be present in your life.

You can embrace your life **now**. Be intentional about your life **now**. Be inspired to being still and focused **now**. Gain more awareness **now**. Take the time **now**. Joy is **now**. Listen to your life **now**. It is speaking to you. What is it saying? It is saying, You have the audacity to desire more joy in your life and deserve to have it **now**.

I'd love to accompany you on this journey. I invite you to sign up for my monthly newsletter at
http://eepurl.com/KPlMn

Chapter 1

Joy is in the Now Place when you…

Don't Wait For a Rainy Day

"Life is not measured by the number of breaths we take but by the moments that take our breath away."-Maya Angelou

"Joy is in the Now Place." What exactly does that mean? Is joy something different than happiness? According to Webster's, joy is a **state** of great delight or satisfaction and happiness means to be pleased or glad over a particular thing. To me, happiness seems to be contingent upon temporary and external situations while **joy is a state of being on the inside**.

Joy is something that you feel no matter what is going on around you. Joy sticks around no matter if you are in, heading towards, or coming out of a storm. I believe joy is more sustainable because of this. I realize there are times when you can be more focused on the past or fret over the future. However, try not to be neglectful of the present.

There is no better time than now. If not now, when? The title, ***Joy is in the Now Place***, means the right now place where your life truly is. Your life is now, not later. It comes from a place inside of you. It is relational. It feels life's movements and rhythm of life. When you check into this "Now Place," it gives moments meaning. You listen to and watch your life. It allows your heart to be open. You are checking in with yourself. You commit to others, now commit to yourself. You are surrendering in the moment. You

9

are discovering the poetry of life. There is wisdom and clarity there. Worry is null and void. There is self-knowledge and self-acceptance there.

In the "Now Place", you are tapping into more love and peace. There is contentment there. There are answers to life there. If you allow yourself to go even deeper into this place, you will discover dancing and laughter there too.

You may say, who needs all of that? Just live your life, right? However, I say, **No**. Living your life is more than just existing. You can experience more meaning from it. I know you may want to go to a higher level in your business and personal life, but it starts with self. Believe it or not, it starts now. You may have heard the phrase, "Yesterday is in the tomb and tomorrow is in the womb but the only important time is now."

So let's move forward in your journey of discovering **"Joy is in the Now Place."**

My defining moments…

I remember my wonderful grandmother, Ida, whom I lovingly called Grammie. She was a hard working woman who worked as a maid and had a limited education. She was so kind to me and I loved being around her. Additionally, I must say, she was a terrific cook. She could take a few ingredients and make a delicious meal. Everything was homemade and never was any "boxed" food items used in Grammie's kitchen. She believed every meal needed a great dessert and, of course, she let me determine what the dessert would be for the meal. I thought that was pretty cool and chocolate anything was great.

We were very close. I remembered the wonderful smells coming from the kitchen; times when I got to sit in her favorite big chair and talk to her for hours about my little old life while eating a pint of Neapolitan ice cream she purchased for me from Walgreens. My Grammie was the best. She was patient and funny too. She would even let me eat the chocolate ice cream out of the center of the ice cream carton. You see, Neapolitan ice cream had 3 flavor blocks: strawberry, vanilla and chocolate. Needless to say, my mom would have never let me scoop out the chocolate and leave the other flavors. No problem with Grammie; she would eat what was left of the pint because she would never let anything go to waste. You might wonder why she did not just buy me a pint of chocolate ice cream instead? To put it briefly, that would just defeat the purpose. It was something special between the two of us that most people might not ever understand (Smile).

My great uncles, when they were serving in the military, had sent Grammie several beautiful nightgowns and elegant embroidered slips from Germany. As a little girl, I thought they were the most precious garments that I had ever seen. However, Grammie never wore them. She always stored them neatly in her top dresser drawer. Grammie said she was waiting to wear them later, maybe on a rainy day. I didn't understand "wait" (like most children). Why was she waiting? Why not now? This did not make sense to a curious child like me. So, periodically, when I was not stirring chocolate cake batter, I would run to her bedroom, get the step stool, and climb to peek into her dresser drawer. I thought it was my duty to check out those beautiful garments and, just as I thought, they were always there, untouched, at least not by her. Folded neatly with white tissue paper between each, they were waiting. How could this be?

In my head, I thought if she did not want to wear them, maybe I could play dress up. I wanted to twirl around and place a book on my head and walk like a model or a princess. Was this over the top? Well…I was around 6 years old at the time. After all, she was not doing anything fun with them. But oh no…Grammie said again, "maybe on a rainy day."

Consequently, my head dropped to my chest and I poked out my bottom lip. Usually, giving Grammie that poor sad face worked. Nonetheless, it did not work in this situation. It was easier giving her that face for an extra brownie before my mother picked me up after work than playing dress up with those garments. Besides, an extra warm brownie worked great for me too.

It had been at least a decade ago since this occurred. I had many wonderful memories racing through my mind of Grammie. I knew I had to snap out of it. I saw the sadness on my mom's face as she packed Grammie's things for her transition to the skilled nursing facility; I had to come back to reality. Grammie was gravely ill. I knew in my heart she was not going to return home. I sat almost frozen. It was one of the saddest days of my life. I could not sit there any longer.

I knew I should have helped my mother pack more but it was too upsetting for me. I could not even imagine the hurt my mom was experiencing. The atmosphere was too quiet and sad.

So, I got up from the chair and walked slowly into Grammie's bedroom. I slowly scanned the room. I took a deep breath as I moved closer to her beautiful dresser. I did not need a step stool this time because I was a college student. I counted 1, 2, 3 as I opened the top drawer and, once again, everything appeared untouched as before, the gowns neatly folded. However, when I unfolded the tissue paper from the first garment (a beautiful embroidered night gown) and tried to hold it up, it literally fell into pieces—it disintegrated right before my eyes. Time stopped! My heart sank and my eyes filled. I felt the warm tears roll down my cheeks. I took another deep breath and headed over to the other side of the room.

It took every part of my being to walk over to the nearby window and not faint. As I got closer, I noticed a few rain drops hitting the window pane. Wow! It was a "rainy day"! This was so ironic. The day was finally here! The day that Grammie spoke of was now too late. She waited too long to enjoy those beautiful garments. On this particular rainy day, she wasn't able to be present to enjoy it. That was so sad. Waiting....

I know this particular experience set into motion for me that "life is now."

Make every effort to stop waiting for another day or another time. Don't wait for a rainy day or even a sunny day to enjoy something or someone. You can't save time. Time is present now to live it, to experience it. Remember **"Joy is in the Now Place".**

What Can I Apply to My Life From This Chapter?

Chapter 2

Joy is in the Now Place when...

The What Ifs Are Not Important

Live in the moment. Again, I realize you have to plan for the future but not at the expense of neglecting or sacrificing the opportunity to be present. Your life is right now. There is so much clarity in the moment! Beauty in the moment! Peace in the moment! Joy in the moment! Less stress in the moment! I believe you can stress more if you focus on the past or focus too much on the future. The would haves, could haves, and should haves, even what ifs, can paralyze you or get you caught in a tail spin.

You may think, why? This behavior can possibly lead you to a huge dose of worry, fear and anxiety. There is absolutely no joy in this. When this happens, you can get distracted and neglect what is happening now, which is your present life. Your life needs your attention. Joy will take reign if you let it. Stay current. Stay focused on the **now**.

My defining moments...

About 20 years ago, I was stressed over leaving my secure corporate career to pursue my own business. Part of the reason I felt stressed was because the many "what ifs" that ran through my mind. What if things don't work out? What if my parents think this is a bad decision? What if this drains us financially? I just didn't want to make a bad decision that would adversely affect my husband and daughter. I had this conversation with my husband many times before, but I wanted to approach him again. I wanted to vent. I was in fear mode--truly spiraling out of control. I felt anxious too. I knew my face showed my worry. Likewise, let us not talk about what was going on with my stomach--full of knots. I was coming up with a lot of scenarios with my husband. Speculations! No facts at all! At my second wind, I was going to hit a home run but my husband interrupted my rant. He told me he was going to take a nap. What? He said he was not going to get into my whirlwind. The nerve of him! I can laugh at the situation now but at that moment I was hot. I was too far in the future. I was not embracing the moment at all. I was so exhausted and I did not realize it at the time.

Apparently, I did not know then what I know now. Fear is a thief. I could have at least taken a nap (Smile). I could have gotten some rest so I could have had more clarity on the situation. I just wasted my energy. I was not productive in the moment. I was just going a thousand miles per hour.

I have learned a valuable lesson--there is so much power in the present. You have to get a hold of your emotions. Yes, your emotions are important but you still have to manage them for your benefit. Take a pause for the cause. When I allow myself to be more present, I feel the joy. Actually, I am bathing in it.

Try it now; experience the present for awhile. How does that feel? Do you feel less anxious? Do you feel less stress? How does your stomach feel right now? Tap into your body. It will take time but if you practice it will become a habit. Even the Bible says, "Give us this day…" I feel there is some relevance there. The only thing you know is now; everything else is pure speculation, especially things in the future. You have enough to be concerned with now. Take good care of each moment of the day as it comes.

You will feel more joy and peace because of it.

What Can I Apply to My Life From This Chapter?

Chapter 3

Joy is in the Now Place when you…

Be Still

As a matter of fact, another Holy Bible Scripture I value is, "Be still and know…." I believe there is so much power in this scripture especially when it is applied. I could have taken the previous situation I have spoken about and sat still, but instead, I chose to spiral out of control. It is certain that we can't change people, but we can change our response to a person or a situation.

When I am present, it allows me to commune with myself. I am in a relationship with a small voice. I'm not anxious. Answers come to me more easily. This world is so noisy. It is saying more and more, faster and faster.

There are many distractions everywhere lobbying for our attention. We are being pulled in many directions. We have to shut off these distractions a little each day. Why? There are many benefits when you do, such as great clarity, answers to your prayers, a mental break, less stress, more focus, more peace.

I know you are probably thinking you are way too busy to "Be Still," but your life deserves it. You can't afford not to.

If I may suggest, try being still each day for 10 minutes. I like starting my day in prayer, reflecting on the Word of God. Next, I sit still for at least ten more minutes, sometimes longer. I feel so much better afterwards. I feel refreshed instead of feeling anxious about the day. You can start with 10 minutes then you can gradually move to 20 minutes. It is really up to you.

My desire for you now is to just start. You do not have to make it complicated. Simplicity is always best. Try it for 30 days. Research shows that if you do something for at least 30 days, it can become a habit. I believe this can be a winning situation. Do not be discouraged when you start.

At the beginning, you may find yourself thinking of your to-do list, grocery list or work projects. Just hang in there; it gets easier. If you allow your mind to be present, your body (behaviors) will follow. I have been a praying person for many years, but there were times when I never sat still long enough to hear an answer or feel the joy on the inside. I was always going on to the next thing.

Like me, you can learn to behave differently. Let the flow take place. Your answer may be a breath away if you allow yourself to "Be Still." Remember we are human-beings not just human-doings.

My defining moments…

One particular day, I remember sitting near my bay window sipping on my favorite rose tea. It had such a pleasant and calming aroma. I thought I was going to finish the entire cup as I took in the scenery from my view. One sip, two sips, several sips then done. I knew I was on my countdown of "Being Still."

Next, I took a couple of deep cleansing breaths in and slowly out through my nose. This felt so cleansing. I remember not being so focused on my surroundings or on that beautiful aroma. I felt myself letting go but where? Oh well…I did not care. I remember it felt great. I was just soaring like an eagle. I did not feel overwhelmed by the burdens of life. I did not have to fix everything and come up with all the answers. Wow this was great!

Then all of a sudden, thoughts came out of nowhere, rushing in: remember to pick up the dry cleaning; did you take out the ground turkey for chili tonight; will my upcoming presentation be good enough or mediocre? Oh my goodness! What happened? Should I stop I thought? No way! So I continued on. I took in more deep cleansing breaths. I did not give up. Those day to day distractions were blocked. They can wait.

I allowed myself to drift. I heard a very small calming voice say, Be still and know all is well. I thought that was so profound. I sighed with relief. I felt so much joy pouring from my heart. My answer was there all along and the only thing I had to do was to be still.

What Can I Apply to My Life From This Chapter?

Chapter 4

Joy is in the Now Place when…

Thoughts Are Seeds
*"Whether you think you can or
you think you can't, you're right."-Henry Ford*

I believe thoughts are seeds just like words are seeds. What thoughts are taking up real estate in your mind? What is going on between your ears? What is your self-talk? How do you feel about yourself? Are you good enough? Is your mind filled with chatter? Is it true? Or is it someone else's opinion of you? Clutter! Clutter! Clutter!

Your body follows your thoughts. If you want to have an indication of what someone is thinking, just check out his or her behaviors.

You have to fill your mind with positive, productive thoughts. For example allow yourself to think the following thoughts regularly: I deserve joy, I want love, I am worthy, I can excel beyond measure, I am successful, and I am healthy.

Once you plant those thoughts then it starts the process. Something starts to happen. Something takes root.

You may say, That sounds great but how do you stop those non-productive thoughts from seeping in? First, you have to be mindful of what you allow into your eye and ear gates. You have to set better boundaries for what you give your attention to. What do I mean? I am glad you asked. Who is in your inner circle of influence? Who is getting into your head space?

I believe if you change your thinking, you can change the direction of your life. If you let negative, rotten messages pile into your thoughts, it can possibly manifest itself in your life. Do you deserve that? Of course not! Are these thoughts adding value or depleting your energy? I like to call these negative thoughts "energy vampires". They could draw the life out of you. What are you listening to? Is it inspiring? Is it uplifting you? If not, reconsider those elements in your life. I believe your output is relative to your input.

The goal is to be present in your life where joy resides. If you want better results plant only positive seeds.

My defining moments…

One fall morning, I was getting ready for work. I was going through my overwhelming mental check list: pack my lunch; fix dinner later; call the teacher; and go visit mom and dad. I had a lot to do with a short amount of time. In addition, I could not forget the Women's Day Ministry to-do list: I needed to send out the emails; follow up with the speakers; and check with the Vice-Chair for any other last minute details. It was truly a litany of "just stuff."

Well of course, I could do it! I had my "Super Woman" cape on with the big red "S" on the back of it. Even though I was complaining all the way, I tried to deceive myself that I could do it all. That was definitely an oxymoron. Either way, figuratively, my cape was tight because I had piled too many things on my plate. Yes, on my own plate. Did someone else pile stuff on my plate? Oh no, I was proud of that pile. Who could not be proud of my plate? It had a variety of things on it, business and personal responsibilities.

Really I was way too busy. Isn't that what I should do? I should be busy every second of the day. Busy is good, right? It looks good to others and maybe on my resume too (Smile).

Yep! I was truly busy but not effective. Certainly, I could add one more thing to my plate but was I present at all? No joy, just busy. No peace, just exhausted. No one gives me a break, I said. Why? Why? I was in my whine moment.

Then, in the mist of my "poor me" episode, I heard the phone ring. Who could this be this early? I wondered. Oh no, I do not need something else to deal with this morning. Finally, I answered the phone. It was my very dear friend, Jeannette, whom I affectionately called Jaye. She was checking to see how I was doing. It was nice of her to call. I wanted to tell her about all the things I had to do later, my woes, of course.

However, I had to stop half way through my own crisis to take a deep breath. You have to know a little about my dear friend, Jaye. Her voice was always so strong, compassionate and filled with joy. You would have never known by her voice and enthusiasm she had been stricken with Muscular Sclerosis (MS) a few years prior and had been bedridden. However, she was always so inspirational. She never complained about her situation and she had good reason to if she wanted to focus on her illness.

That was why I decided to stop complaining about my day. I took my eyes off myself and changed my focus. Jaye had in her usual generous spirit asked me how I was doing and how she could help me. Wow! That was so touching, I thought. It was a teachable moment for me. If she could find joy in her situation then I certainly could too. She encouraged me to live in the present, not necessarily with her words, but how she embraced her life, loved her family and friends and had a lot of joy. I believe it was no accident that she even named her daughter, Joi. She decided to live in love and not bitterness about her illness. She made a conscious effort to love every aspect of her life.

Our friendship was priceless. I am grateful our lives crossed. I was once told it does not matter how long you live but how you live it and care for others. That is the wonderful part about the "dash in the middle" between your birth date and the date you transcend from your earthly life. It is all about how you affect others to want to be better.

Her life was a true testimony to live in the present and not take her life for granted.

Every moment is so precious. I truly miss my friend, Jaye, a lot but I am reminded of those grateful and joyful lessons she demonstrated for me.

Do you have a special relationship that positively affects your life? What life lessons are you gaining? Take this time to reflect. What brings you joy about the person or situation? You can write about it or draw a special memory here.

What Can I Apply to My Life From This Chapter?

Chapter 5

Joy is in the Now Place when you...

Celebrate Now
*"The more you praise and celebrate your life,
the more there is in life to celebrate."-Oprah Winfrey*

Celebrate **now**! Dance **now**! Love **now**! Start your
Business **now**! Watch a sunrise or sunset **now**! Write
your book **now**! You can fill in your own blanks. What
are you waiting for? Consider not putting things off
until later. Later may never come. All you have is right
now. Take a deep breath and embrace it. Accept life
now. Life is precious and fleeting. Do not squander
your time.

How, you may ask? As I had mentioned before, by
being stuck in the past or being lost too far in the
future, you lose those precious moments.

Who says we have to celebrate only the traditional
times: birthdays, anniversaries and holidays? Create
your own times to celebrate. What about "just
because" celebrations: just because you are alive,
just because you received a great doctor's report, just
because you received all the money you need to put a
down payment on a new home and on and on.

Your celebration does not need to be grandiose; it is
about taking the time to be grateful and be in the
moment. It is all about taking great care of you. **It is
not selfish to take care of you.** Others benefit too.
You do not need anyone's permission to celebrate.

You can have a party of one. When was the last time you took yourself out to lunch or dinner? Do not let your life get too chaotic that you lose yourself. Take the time. Also you can invite others to your celebration. You gain joy when you celebrate. When you celebrate moments, you usher in the attitude of gratefulness.

What a time for splendor! Have you watched children? Children know how to celebrate. They know how to wave their hands in the air, laugh and have a good time, even if others are watching. Children know how to have a little cake icing on their lips and not be totally horrified. They are okay if they have a hair out of place. Children make me laugh when I am around them. I love the sounds they make too. It makes me smile and sometimes laugh. They are so carefree and fun, knowing how to embrace every single moment. Usually, children are not overly concerned about what is going to happen two weeks from now. They will even skip if they want to get somewhere faster. Children know how to have joy.

But what happened? I believe they learned how to calm or quiet their expressions over time. This can be good at times but as they grow, somewhere along the line, they become stifled. Now, as an adult, we take life way too seriously.

So how do you get your joy back? How do you celebrate your life more? You have to **decide** you want more laughter, to be more lighthearted and to have more joy. If you think that is important to you then it becomes a priority. Who wants to be around a person who is too serious and uptight all the time?

Celebrate **now**; do not wait until later. Give yourself a break. You deserve it and the people around you do too. *Joy awaits you.*

My defining moments…

Go with me here. It was not too long ago, my husband and I were in the lower level of our home. My husband is a huge music lover (of all kinds). He has an amazing music collection. On this particular evening, he went over to his vinyl collection. Some may call this the "old school" collection, his long playing albums (LP's). He went over to his record player and turned it on. Yes, I did say record player. I was sitting on the chaise taking this all in--just enjoying the moment. It was my relaxing time.

Indeed, my husband was getting strategic, contemplating which album to select. "Oh…this one," he said and carefully removed the shiny vinyl album from the jacket. He spun it around with his hands, blew off a little dust, and placed it on the spindle. Next, he moved the needle arm carefully onto the album after deciding the specific song he thought I wanted to hear. Careful! Easy does it! Please do not scratch the album.

Here it goes. Those easy grooving sounds filled the air. You could not help but take it in. Before we knew it, we started snapping our fingers and swaying. "Would you like to dance darling?" he said. Before he could finish his sentence, I was up on my feet and ready. I never turn down a dance. We were slow dancing. It was so much fun.

Just as he was about to spin me around and possibly give me a little dip backwards, our daughter came downstairs. We heard her say, "Really, mom and dad, really?" We both looked at her and she had that horrified look on her face that most young people get when they think their parents are doing something that is totally out of their league. She said she could not believe we were still dancing after all these years.

Well, my husband and I had the biggest kick out of that because we never stopped dancing. Why did she ever think that? I told her we were taking the time to enjoy the moment, celebrating the "now". Our daughter snickered and just shook her head. She said, "Ok, Dad, but you only have **one** good dance move." He said, "That may be true, but I only need **one** good dance move that works. That's all it takes." He spun me around again and gave me that smooth backwards dip. Our daughter threw up her hands and left the room. We both said, "Touchdown."

What Can I Apply to My Life From This Chapter?

Chapter 6

Joy is in the Now Place when…

Laughter is Healing

You have to laugh more and not take life so seriously. As I see it, laughter is healing. Granted, everywhere we turn there are disasters and hurts but there is still hope. Yes, life can weigh you down but take a deep breath and try to lighten up more.

According to the Mayo Clinic Staff, laughter is a great form of stress relief. Here are a few benefits listed from their article, "Stress Relief from Laughter? It's no Joke."

Benefits:
When you laugh, it just does not lighten your load mentally; it actually induces physical changes in your body.

Stimulates Many Organs:
Laughter enhances your intake of oxygen-rich air, which stimulates your heart, lungs and muscles and increases the endorphins that are released by your brain.

Soothes Tension:
Laughter can stimulate circulation and aid muscle relaxation, which can reduce some physical symptoms of stress.

Improves your immune system:
Negative thoughts can manifest into chemical reactions that can affect your body by bringing on more stress into your system and decreasing your immunity. In contrast, positive thoughts actually

release neuropeptides, which can help fight stress and potentially more serious illnesses.
(Mayo Clinic 2013)

Laughter can elevate your mood. I believe laughter can help you to cope with the stresses of life. I love a deep hearty laugh especially about something I did. Sometimes I laugh so hard it brings tears to my eyes. This probably is too corny but I even love a good "knock-knock" joke.

Good clean laughter is a must for me. What about you? I do not have to schedule laughter, but it comes out easily for me because I try not to be too hard on myself. I know if I am not hard on myself then I can do the same for others. If you take yourself too seriously, it can make you more stressed. Who needs more of that? Loosen up!

Laughter is a choice. How? Check out who you hang out with? Are they easygoing people who love to have fun? If not, add some new friends. Look at some old photos that might give a few good chuckles. Go to the park or beach. Look at the children having a good time. Attend a good clean comedy show. Hilarious! Go with some friends. Start smiling more. Rent or buy some funny movies.

After you have a good hearty laugh, tap into how you are feeling. Do you feel less tense? How do your muscles feel? Do you feel lighter? If not, you are not laughing enough. Let yourself go. I have never heard of a good hearty laugh hurting anyone. Get started.

My defining moments...

So I remember spending time at my favorite used book store. It has droves and droves of great books. I can get lost looking sometimes, but on this particular day, I saw the perfect little book. It was a Disney joke book. Who knew? I thought this would be a great book for my little friend, Fisher. He was such a neat little boy, but he did not laugh much. From what he had shared previously, he had many family issues. His parents struggled financially and there was not much money to go around-especially for fun things. He seemed sad most of the time. I wanted to get him something that could cheer him up and that he could carry around with him. I could not wait to give it to him the next time I saw him.

A few days later, I saw Fisher. I pulled my surprise out of my book bag. His eyes lit up. I asked if I could read it to him and he said, Cool. At the same time, he gave me the look out of the corner of his eye with that cute half grin. I knew he was trying to hold back his excitement. This is a Disney joke book and I bought it especially for you, I said. As I started reading the jokes, I immediately started laughing and he did the same. I was glad to see him happy instead of sad. Then he said hearing me laugh was funnier than the jokes. He said it was funny seeing an adult laugh so much.

Fisher reminded me there was not a lot of laughter in his home. However, I did not try to press him on what else was going on in his home, even though, I suspected more. I saw him several times after that and we spent each time just laughing, not being concerned about stressful things but just having fun.

In these experiences with my little friend, Fisher, I believe laughter was healing for him. I saw him evolve from a sad little boy to a little boy with a sparkle of joy in his eyes. I believe we healed each other.

Laughter is contagious. You can learn to have more fun. It is never too late. I believe laughter is good medicine; it is priceless, and easy to share. There is joy in laughter. Do not wait. Give yourself permission to chuckle now. If you start laughing now and if someone is around you, chances are they will start laughing too. Give it a try.

What Can I Apply to My Life From This Chapter?

Chapter 7

Joy is in the Now Place when...

Eating Without Distractions

Do you allow yourself to eat without distractions? What do I mean? In my opinion, when I take the time to eat without background chatter—watching television, checking my emails or getting the latest social media scoop—I enjoy my meal better. I know I eat less and feel more satisfied.

According to the article, "Distracted Eating May Add to Weight Gain" by Howard LeWine, M.D., he states, "Multitasking—like eating while watching television or working—and distracted or hurried eating can prompt you to eat more. Slowing down and savoring your food can help you control your intake." (LeWine 2013)

Another report published in the *American Journal of Clinical Nutrition* looked at how food intake affects attention and memory. A study was conducted using two groups eating meals, one while watching television and the other without television. The studies had two key conclusions:

> First, being distracted while eating a meal tended to make people eat more at the meal; and second, paying attention to the meal was linked to eating less in the future. (American Journal of Clinical Nutrition 2013)

I try to make a conscious effort when I eat not to be on the computer or even on my cell phone.

At that moment, after I bless my food (grateful for the day and the nourishment), I love taking in all the food colors—red, green, yellow—as well as the different shapes. Oh my, let us not forget about the different smells—citrus, tangy, sweet, spicy etc. I just do not want to rush eating. I try to allocate enough time. Why? It helps to minimize digestive concerns such as gas, bloating or heartburn. I try to savor every small bite.

Trust me, this may seem like a process but it does not take a lot of time. It is so rewarding. Just try it. You will find that it takes less time to eat when you do not have all those distractions. In my experience, this is what has contributed to my eating fewer calories and getting satisfied more quickly. I enjoy the entire eating experience, not just the food.

Would you try this on your next meal? Turn off all distractions-no checking your emails and social media posts. It can wait for 20 minutes or so (Smile). Take in all the aspects and be present. It's wonderful, right?

My defining moments…

I was standing in the middle of my kitchen thinking about the night's dinner. I thought we had been doing the same old thing for a while. I wanted for the family to have more togetherness. What is the point? Maybe my daughter would think that mom is getting too strict. She has been in the health care field too long and now she is bringing this stuff home. Mom has lost her mind.   I kept rehearsing the scenarios over and over. The "what ifs" were trying to creep in. Dinner is done, everything is in place, and it is a week night, I said. No real big surprise; it was a planned meal, which saved a lot of time and money too.

It was Mexican Dinner Night: grilled chicken fajitas, black beans, Spanish rice, homemade salsa, guacamole and garnishments: cilantro, red onions, sliced limes and jalapenos. So what was the problem as I looked around the room? I have to do something different, I thought. Hm…I have an idea. Thirty minutes later, everyone came in on time from work and school, washed their hands and got ready for dinner.

Everything was normal on the surface. I was glad about my new surprise. Before I could say a word my daughter said, Oh no! Where is the television? Was it stolen? This is a travesty. My husband had the same look of distain on his face. This was unheard of to do something like this (Smile). Why was the television taken out of the kitchen? Who does this? We did not have a family meeting about this? We always look at our favorite programs while we eat.

Before, everyone had been so engaged in the programs that we had little time to share with each other, a good old-fashioned conversation. My husband, who is such a fast eater, would be finished and gone from the table to sit in front of the big screen television downstairs. I shared with my family that having the television in the kitchen was too distracting to our family and the meal. We could spend our time sharing about our day with each other. I thought we needed more quality time together. Also, I thought my husband would be impressed with the idea. We would eat fewer calories if the television was not in the kitchen. He was not buying into that. Well…needless to say, there was not a lot of communicating during that particular meal.

However, I am proud to say the television never returned to the kitchen and we communicated more with each other. It was such a small adjustment; at least I thought, but they got used to it. In fact, we embraced more goodness about the food too. It is amazing—same people and the same food—but we took the time to notice.

How important is that to you? You might not do something as drastic but there are many ways to connect and be present with your family. It is priceless! Capture the moment! Make a slight shift and you will gain great benefits.

I even removed the television from our bedroom. I will tell you about the benefits of that in my next book (Smile).

What are some slight changes you can make to communicate better with your family?

Are there any distractions you can minimize or remove?

What Can I Apply to My Life From This Chapter?

Chapter 8

Joy is in the Now Place when you...

Get Out Of Your Own Way
"Our deepest fear is not that we are inadequate.
Our deepest fear is that we are
powerful beyond measure."-Marianne Williamson

We have to move out of our own way. Sometimes we are the blockers.

Wow! I did say that. That is too deep to say. I think it is easier to blame others but if you can become more present about your life, you will be amazed at the results. If your thoughts are circulating around, you may want to change the continuous loop in your mind.

The "Now Place" is the truth. How? It is not about what your past has to say or the fears of the future. Have you heard the phrase that FEAR stands for False Evidence Appearing Real? Fear is an energy drainer. Fear can keep you stuck or even paralyze.

When you get out of your own way and allow life, I believe exceptional blessings take place. No need to be hesitant. It is almost like asking for an overflow of blessings to come into your life but you start building a wall, a hedge. Now does that make sense? In my opinion, no!

You do not short circuit your life's potential by allowing negative thoughts, negative people or even yourself to get in the way. You may say your finances are awful, your children are acting out, the rent or mortgage is due, you are in a dead-end job and your marriage has problems. While all of this may be true, this is where your faith should come in. You have to believe things will get better. Your children may be watching your response to life too.

My mother used to say there is always someone else worse off and be grateful for where you are now. I am not diminishing your situation and it may be hard right now but things usually get better. As long as you have breath in your body, add a little strength and mix in a little faith; you can make it. I believe a little hope goes a long way too. Hold on! Do not give up! Keep one foot in front of the other. Keep walking. There were times in my life I fell flat on my face but each time I kept getting up. Tap inside for the strength to get up. Dust yourself off. I encourage you to have the attitude that you refuse to be defeated. It can be just your perspective or response to the situation.

I know the hardest times in my life have brought out the best in me. Yes, it did not feel great "going through" it, but it taught me some great life lessons. They were the perfect lessons for moving to my next level in life. You will go through some tough times in your life but the operative word is "through." It means you will not stay there.

Do not block your blessings. Experience the joy. Serve better. Expect better. Do better. Embrace better.

My defining moments...

It was not too long ago that, I was talking with Cooper, an acquaintance of mine, who was having a really rough time in his life, even to despair. He kept telling me the situations in his life confirmed to him that everything would remain the same. He had lost four jobs and had a couple of dead-end relationships. Cooper was determined that his life was never going to get better. He continued to play the same thoughts out in his head. He was not short on vocalizing this on a regular basis too.

In my opinion, I believe every cell in his body heard him, loud and clear. His actions confirmed his thoughts. It seemed like an endless loop. Cooper even said, I know I am in my own way but I have proof with all the failed attempts and disappointments to prove it. Could it be he was perpetuating these negative results by his thoughts? I felt this could be a contributor.

I believe we can partner in our own results. In all honesty, there were some difficult situations in my life where I truly participated in causing them, and I can say I did a good job at it too. There were times I knew I was not living up to my potential and wanted to blame others for it. I had the negative self-talk going on in my thoughts, until I decided I wanted and deserved better in my life. The change had to start in my thoughts.

I really like the phrase, Change your thinking; Change your life. There has to be a connection to this, a definite link. If I could see your thoughts, you might be thinking, "Yes, I can change my thoughts and get out of my own way but bad things still can happen." You are so correct. There are many situations that can happen we can't control. Be that as it may, I believe we can change our response to the situation.

When I reflect over my life, there were situations I could not control such as the death of my parents, car accidents, other disappointments; however, there were many situations that I participated in, initiated and even stood in my own way. Usually there was no one to blame but me. Even though I did try to point fingers. Nonetheless, I still have to chalk it up to situations that made me who I am today. I did not allow myself to get stuck or even dwell there. I did not want to use these situations to give me permission to block my own way or someone else's way too.

So you may say this sounds interesting but how does a person know if he/she is standing in their own way? Well, first do you feel stuck or stagnant? Are you progressing? Do you feel joy in your life? Are opportunities passing you by?

Here is another important question. How do you move past this situation?
The list below is not extensive but it can give you some basic suggestions.

- Admit that you may be blocking your progression
- Pray/meditate

- Seek counseling
- Hire a Life Coach
- Be present
- Journal
- Walk in faith not fear
- Get a support system
- Set realistic goals
- Practice better nutrition
- Receive Massage Therapy
- Get restful sleep
- Exercise

Reminder: You are not alone on this journey. For additional information and more practical suggestions, I invite you to sign up for my monthly newsletter at **http://eepurl.com/KPIMn**

What Can I Apply to My Life From This Chapter?

Chapter 9

Joy is in the Now Place when you…

Aim, Balance and Dismount Well

Everyone has had, at some time, the challenge of balancing certain aspects of their lives. If you have not, my mother always said, please keep living. It eventually will happen. You may feel you are being pulled in several different directions. It sometimes can feel like you are in a tug of war and you are not quite sure who is going to win. You feel like you are being pulled between your personal life and career, community projects and work, your spouse and your children.

How do you balance it so you will not feel guilty because you are spending more time with one over the other? If you spend more time with your career/business, then your family life can suffer or vice versa. How can you feel more balanced? Can you have it all? Good questions, right?

First, you have to determine what "all" is for you. No one can figure that out but you. Once again, you have to sit still to be present in the moment. You have to ask yourself what is truly important to you. What makes sense? Not what the media says or statistics say about your life. What is at your core? What do you feel in your belly? What makes your heart skip a beat? Allow yourself to be realistic and do not cheat yourself. This is a very crucial step. You can't prioritize or balance your life if you do not have a clue of what is important.

If you say everything you are doing is important, then I will beg to differ. There are probably one, two or many things you are doing that may not be necessary for your journey. When I did some housecleaning of my own life, I determined there were many things that were not conducive to the success of my life such as: always saying yes to someone else's agenda; not resting enough; and spending too much time with energy draining people. Given that, I had to move some things around and even clear some things out—including people. It was the hardest thing to do but necessary in the long run. Additionally, this housecleaning process is seasonal and ongoing.

Second, after you have clearly determined who or what is important, then you need balance. You have to realistically determine how much time is needed for each part of your life. Do not put too much pressure on your shoulders doing this. For example, when my daughter was younger, I needed to spend more time with her, especially, during her formative years, but as she grew into a young woman, she needed less of my time. I knew that quality time and being fully present was and is the golden key.

Third, in order to balance your life, you need to keep a basic routine/schedule for your life. It does not have to be huge. You can have a very basic schedule but it is necessary to be consistent. Just because you have room to add one more thing on your plate, you don't have to fill it--that goes for eating more food or adding another project. When you have a routine or schedule, I believe it minimizes frustration and stress. For me, in the morning when I am given the gift of opening my eyes and being present, I pray, meditate and exercise. That is my routine. What is yours?

Last, learn to say "no" when needed. The word "no" is a complete answer. It does not need an explanation unless you give one. Say no especially when saying yes is going to overwhelm you or does not add value to your life.

Also, set up good boundaries for your life. The opposite of chaos is balance and organization. It can happen now and watch your joy flow in.

My defining moments...

It seems like yesterday but it was almost twenty years ago, gymnast, Kerri Strug, despite the odds, helped the U.S. win a gold medal at the Atlanta Olympics. She was a member of the Magnificent Seven, the victorious all around women's gymnastics team. Kerri is best known for her amazing vault performance. Prior to this accomplishment, she had injured her ankle from a very difficult vault that required a handspring and a twisting dismount. However, she slipped when she landed, fell backwards and snapped her left ankle. The crowd roared and I gasped with disbelief too. My heart went out for Kerri. I knew she was in great pain. Her score flashed on the board, 9.162.

The U.S. Women's Gymnastics Team had never won a gold medal before. Just like the other fans, I thought this would happen again--no gold. In the meantime, her coach, Bela Karolyi, walked over to her, gave her a hug, said a few words and lifted her to her feet. The crowd was going nuts and I was too. Could I be seeing things? Was she going for a second attempt? Was the U.S. getting another opportunity for a gold medal?

I literally had to hold my breath as she got in position for her second and final vault. It seemed she had to have been in excruciating pain. However, Kerri got in position, took a deep breath and sprinted down the runway as fast as she could. I was jumping up and down and screaming at the television. Go, Kerri go! Kerri leaped high in the air, did a back handspring on the vault perfectly.

Everyone was bracing themselves because of the pain she was going to experience when she landed on that damaged ankle. I knew that had taken a lot of determination, courage and strength. Kerri landed very hard on her feet and did not stumble. She kept her feet balanced, raised her arms long enough for the judges and gave a proud smile. She did it! The Georgia Dome was going crazy: hugging, crying, shouting and lots of "high fives." The awesome Kerri Strug earned a 9.712 score which gave the U.S. a gold medal over the shocked Russian athletes. It was the first time since 1948 the Soviet Union team did not win a gold medal.

When young Kerri was asked later where did she get her strength and what was she thinking during this time she said, "Please God, help me with this vault. I have done this a thousand times. I know I can do it one more time, injured ankle or not."

This was another defining moment for me. It is amazing how disciplined the mind is when you get focused and the body will respond accordingly. I am not saying it takes an injured ankle, pushing yourself to those limits but I am saying if you get out of the way of barriers, many great things can happen. You are so powerful. You can do incredible things too. When struggles or difficult times come, you can go beyond them. You can vault over them.

As I see it, you have to get focused, pray and believe.
Persevere! Aim high! Expect the best! Balance!
Dismount well and always give thanks!

Have you ever been in a situation where it seemed like the odds were against you? Did you triumph? If yes, what or who helped you? What strengths did you acquire from this situation? List them below or take time to be still and reflect on them.

1.
2.
3.
4.
5.
6.

What Can I Apply to My Life From This Chapter?

Chapter 10

Joy is in the Now Place when you...

Repurpose, If Necessary

I admit **"repurpose"** is one of my new words for this season. Yes, I am one of those people who gets a particular word landed in my spirit and I have to see how it takes root and plays out in my life.

According to Webster's dictionary, repurpose means to adapt for use in a different purpose. Wow! That really radiates with me. How cool is that? To change something so that it can be used for a different purpose. The audacity to have that kind of courage is astonishing! If necessary, I am convinced you can change a particular aspect of yourself to be used for a different purpose. This is so wonderful because you can forever be evolving. It means nothing is wasted, just repurposed. Every part of you has meaning and can be used in other ways too. If your life seems boring, unfulfilled and it lacks joy, think of ways you can repurpose it.

Repurpose is not just for repurposing furniture, metal or wood. You can always view your life through a different lens. As you go through your day, keep looking for ways to repurpose. You can take one of your talents, skills or passion and repurpose it for a different use. This can give you more joy, more freedom and a new level of life.

My defining moments...

Another way I like to spend my "me time" is to watch DIY (Do It Yourself) channels or home fixer upper programs. I gain a lot of insight, always a teachable moment.

I recall Chip and Joanna Gaines, HGTV Fixer Upper program, shopping at a vintage salvage store. There was a clunky piece of stone sitting in the corner with a unique design ingrained in it. At my initial glance, it looked really odd. It seemed useless and unattractive but it caught my eye anyway during the television program. However, the renovators walked past it looking at beautiful shiny things instead. I remember thinking, what was that odd looking thing? Why was it in the camera's view? It really did not flow with the scenery. Then all of a sudden, the camera panned back to this odd piece because the renovators walked towards it.

Joanna said, Look at this unique piece. What do you think it is? Chip said, that he did not know what it was but he went over to it and wiped off the dust. The more he wiped, he discovered it was marble. Joanna said, I just love it! I do not know what we can use it for at this time but its purpose will show up.

Fast forward several weeks, the Gaines were showing the house to the new buyers, who were blown away by the beautiful bathroom. The wife was so amazed at the marble vanity counter top. It was reshaped and polished. The wife said she fell more in love with the house because of the fine details of the bathroom, especially the vanity top. Joanna said the counter top was **repurposed** for the special bathroom and the unique design they wanted for them.

I was overly impressed myself. Chip and Joanna did not know the original purpose or use of this dusty, odd shaped stone but they repurposed it for something so amazing. At that very moment, I heard that word, it was a light bulb experience for me. Then I thought, how can I take this wonderful example and apply it to my own life? There were so many ideas racing in my head that I had to get my journal to expound on it. How can I repurpose some areas or skills in my life?

You can do it too. Here is one of my ideas. Since, I love to write and journal personally now I can expand and repurpose my writing skills to include writing books, workbooks, self-help guides, blogs and coaching tools to help empower and inspire others. I was told on many occasions by my husband to write blogs and possibly to write a book. However, I thought he was trying to keep me from talking to him as much (Smile).

Even our good friend, Leon, asked me when I was going to write a book. I thought, how did Leon know I repurposed my writing skills to include a book? This was more confirmation that I was on the right track. Each week at church, I would see Leon and he would always encourage me (during the process) to keep putting pen to paper and call me his "author" friend. It was so surreal how all of this came together. Another friend, Darice, who is great with online/social media marketing, has been inspiring during this journey too. I have learned if you allow the process, you will be given what you need. You have to be willing.

I want you to try this for yourself. This will be an eye-opening experience for you. There is joy everywhere you turn. You have all the resources and skills to be more joyful and successful in your business and personal life. You just have to get started and be consistent. Remember your purpose or repurpose in life is much bigger than you can ever imagine.

Here is your exercise. Go to the next page and subtitle it: **How Can I Repurpose Some Areas or Skills in my Life?** Below the subtitle, on the left column, list all your skills, strengths and passions; on the right column, write out the ways you can repurpose them. I know you will be pleasantly surprised. Take your time. Do not rush through it. It will be an ongoing process.

If you will lend yourself to the process, your life will give glory and be of great service to you and so many others.

What Can I Apply to My Life From This Chapter?

Chapter 11

Joy is in the Now Place when...

Forgiveness Is a Must
*"I am not a product of my circumstances.
I am a product of my decisions."-Stephen Covey*

Even though I debated on adding the delicate subject of forgiveness to my book, I affirm it still has merit here. As I see it, I believe it is so challenging to even consider joy if you are carrying around lots of hurts and pains. Therefore, I believe it necessary to at least shine a little light on this matter. Granted, this information is by no means comprehensive or expert advice necessarily, but hopefully it will bring about some thoughts and considerations. In my opinion, the word "forgiveness" sounds easy but actually the practice can be very overwhelming, stressful, and even frightening.

According to the dictionary, forgiveness means to stop feeling angry or resentful toward someone for an offense, abuse, flaw or mistake. You may have been hurt or abused deeply by a person who should have cared for, nurtured or protected you; however, in the long run, if you continue to carry this around it can burden you. It is possible that being unforgiving can lead to more stress, resentment, hopelessness, rage and depression in your life.

According to the American Psychiatric Association (APA), there is contemporary and compelling

behavioral research on the meaning, process, and the positive effects of forgiveness.
(APA Forgiveness Research 2006)

Forgiveness does not necessarily mean reconciliation. Forgiving someone does not mean that what he or she did was okay or that you gave them permission. Forgiveness merely lets you off the hook of being angry or resentful.

One analogy I have heard is that being unforgiving is like taking poison yourself but wishing the other person would die.

I think in some ways being unforgiving can block closure and you can become like stagnant water that eventually can become toxic. Furthermore, it can suck out all the positive energy in your life. It is like carrying a huge boulder around your neck. You can feel weighed down and you could become unproductive. Have you ever thought it can be like being victimized twice--once by the victor and once by you because you are carrying this around? Holding it affects your life.

Besides, being unforgiving, you can potentially harbor hatred which can lead to rage or even revenge. It perpetuates more pain. It can make it harder for you to heal when this takes place. Being unforgiving does not stay self-contained. The pain or the remnants can affect other people.

How? If you are not being your best self, depressed, counterproductive, and negative, it can spread to others. I am not saying this is intentional; many times it is not. It can hold you back from being fully present, open and loving in your life because of the fear of being hurt again. Nonetheless, the people around you, who had nothing to do with your hurt can likely feel rejected and not know why.

Above all, give your permission to yourself to heal fully.

My defining moments…

According to Andrea Brandt, Ph.D. to determine what forgiveness is not, she offers the following:

- Forgiveness does not mean you are pardoning or excusing the other person's actions.
- Forgiveness does not mean you need to tell the person that he or she is forgiven.
- Forgiveness does not mean you should not have any more feelings about the situation.
- Forgiveness does not mean there is nothing further to work out in the relationship or that everything is okay now.
- Forgiveness does not mean you should forget the incident ever happened.
- Forgiveness does not mean you have to continue to include the person in your life.

(Brandt 2014)

Here is more good news: the joy you deserve awaits you. Truly everyone can stand a little more joy in their lives. I believe when you forgive you are freeing up space in your heart and mind. It is like a computer hard drive that needs more space to add more good information. Further, it allows you to grow more in positive ways. You will not feel hostage to your negative thoughts or anger any longer. You can feel free like an eagle. You are ready to soar. Nothing and no one is holding you back. The life you have on earth is so finite. You have to give yourself permission to feel free and experience the joy. Trust me; I know it is easier said than done. However, I do believe all things are possible with effort and help.

According to the Focus on the Family, Forgiveness and Restoration series by Rose Sweet, "If you do not forgive you are giving the victor control over your life. Forgiving is not the same as forgetting. Forgiveness does not mean you have to pretend it did not happen or you have to run from it."
(Sweet 2001)

If you let that marinate in your heart, I believe you can move towards forgiveness. You have to admit to the pain. If you store it away, it can manifest itself in other ways.

Here are some questions to consider:

What happens if the person says they do not need your forgiveness or won't admit to the pain, abuse or the offense they caused?
Well...forgiving the offender does not necessarily have anything directly to do with him or her. What? I know you are thinking that sounds bizarre. Ok, but let me finish this thought. You can forgive someone without going to them face to face. You forgiving the person has to do with your own anger, and the resentment you have towards them that might be holding you back.

What happens if the person who hurt or abused you is deceased? Can you go to them? Of course not! However, that does not mean you can't still forgive them so you can heal and move forward. You are accepting that this happened to you. However, you are finding a resolution to it. You are not allowing yourself to be bound by it. Also you know that forgiveness is a process that takes time. You can't fully forgive someone until you fully identify, feel it, and release your pain and anger.

I was talking to my friend, Lexi, who was very concerned that the person who hurt her by gossiping about her behind her back would not admit to the offense. I said, If it is important for you to approach her about the offense, then you can't be attached to the outcome. Meaning, you can't control someone else's behavior. You can only control your own reactions. Be mindful that the goal is for you to get free through forgiveness. This has to be about you.

If it is a family member who hurt you, it really makes it super hard. Long ago, I had a similar experience with someone, whom I decided to forgive, even though this person never admitted to the pain that was inflicted on me. I decided to love this person the way God loved this person. I am speaking from my vantage point. I realize that you do not have to have direct contact with the offender to forgive him or her. Again, forgiveness does not necessarily mean reconciliation or confrontation. For me, it was vital that I forgave because the hurt was taking up too much space in my life. I kept rehearsing it in my head and saying, why would this person treat me this way? Why? Why? Why? It really had me stuck far too long. This person was living their life and not realizing or caring about the aftermath.

However, it's been said, Jesus surely did not forgive us without it costing Him dearly. For me, it was a sacrifice to forgive this person but in the long run, it had a great benefit to my life. I am a witness. You can let go of the grudges, grievances and allow yourself to heal. It is really about you and not the offender.

So what happens if the person you need to forgive is you? How does that work? There are many ways but let me start simply. First, you have to recognize you need to be forgiven. I realize that is like taking a big dose of castor oil. It is hard to get down at first, but when it gets down, it does the body wonders. It is healthy to take responsibility and ownership of your behaviors. It is so easy to look at others and pick them to shreds on what is wrong with them. However, one of the true tests of maturity is when we can take a look at our own lives. There are times when we need to go deep within ourselves but, if that is too hard, do not go alone; get yourself an accountability partner or support team to help. This may not be easy but it can be necessary. There are many things or people on the line that need the best out of you.

Second, you have to believe you deserve to be forgiven and let yourself off the hook. This is where your moral and spiritual beliefs can be applied. As you work towards forgiving yourself, you have to totally surrender and be humbled. No more excuses or cover-ups.

Third, there has to be sincerity. You have to be sorry and remorseful. It is possible to say this to yourself while you are looking in the mirror. Be mindful that this is a process. Freeing yourself will not happen overnight and it can take help from others. A couple of my fitness trainer friends have said, in any process, you have to break down the muscle before you can build it back up. There are layers to get through. So that is why humility is a very valuable component in this process.

I believe, in order to move freely in your life and capture more joy, you have to forgive yourself and, if needed, forgive others. Forgiveness is very powerful. It is just like a muscle, the more you use it, the stronger it gets.

Why is it so hard to forgive ourselves? There are several reasons but one that comes to mind is that it is easier to hold on to the anger because it is like a protective coating. Often it seems easier to hold on to the anger than risk the trust required to forgive. It can open old wounds. It can be scary. There is a lot of pride swallowing too. Forgiveness comes from the heart not just from the lips. Remember, you have to be willing to forgive and it can take time. When you are ready, you will know. Forgiveness is a valuable way to honor yourself. You will still remember what happened to you but forgiveness can take away the sting of that memory. You are no longer bound by it.

Release those negative emotions to make room for more joy to come into your life.

"Darkness cannot drive out darkness; only light can do that. Hate cannot drive out hate; only love can do that."-
Dr. Martin Luther King, Jr.

What Can I Apply to My Life From This Chapter?

Chapter 12

Joy is in the Now Place when...

If Not Now, When?

The word "when" seems so far off, compared to "now." Sometimes it is in the distant future. Why is **Now** not a good time? For the people who are waiting around, who and what are you waiting for? Could this be the case--you wait for a lot of things: wait to start a business, wait for someone to pat you on the back; wait for someone else to know how great you are; and wait for someone to give you permission to proceed? Stop it!

If I asked why not now, you probably could provide me a list of why not now's, but as I see it, that is only an excuse. So do not throw any cyber tomatoes at me (Smile). From my experience, I am speaking the truth because I have been there more than once, even in one day.

Certainly, we all have to-do lists and demands. But consider this, I am asking you to add your name to the list, preferably at the top. **Now** is the time to start a better eating plan; **now** is the time to lose those 10 pounds or whatever you have been putting off, **now** is the time to spend more quality time with your family; **now** is the time to start saving for that relaxing vacation. Quit allowing procrastination to be a habit. Why not now?

You can't save time for a later date. Time has to be used now. Time goes by so quickly. Life is important and now. If I asked you what time is it now, I guarantee you will not give me the time five hours from now. You would give the time right now.

Your life is not graded on a curve. It is definitive and finite on earth. You can't just wish for things to get better. If you choose, you can decide on actively participating in your life now. Okay, you may say you have wasted a lot of time. Indeed, that may be the case, but you can't do anything about the past. Acknowledge it and move forward. You have the power **now**! Your joy is **now** and you can start from where you are.

To emphasize, everything can start the moment you decide that **now** is the best and only time. Let there not be another missed opportunity to be present.

My defining moments…

It was a hot summer day. My mother had come to visit for a few days. Wow, three generations under the same roof and remarkably in the same kitchen soon too. It was Saturday and I had lots of chores to do: grocery shopping, laundry, dusting, you name it. I enjoyed my mom coming but I knew I had to get started on my chores. I kept thinking I have to keep my routine: take the laundry downstairs, start sorting whites, colors, stripes. I had it down to a science. My mother asked if she could help but I said I can do it. It will just take a little bit of time. In went the first load of laundry into the washer. I had this under control. This was a cinch. In fact, I would be done in no time.

My mom and I were having a great conversation in the process. She was getting me up to date on what was going on in our hometown, the neighborhood, and our family. I must point out, we talked quite frequently by phone and I knew most of this stuff anyway. In all honesty, I certainly enjoyed our time together. I listened to whom she saw at the Post Office last week, what the butcher said about the special cut of Hoosier ribeye steaks she likes to buy for my dad, and why she can't understand why my dad sits for hours reading all those newspapers (which he has done for 30+ years). Mom pointed out that this is why she enrolled in college--to get a degree in Computer Technology. I told her on many occasions, I was so proud of her for attending college.

She was doing this for herself and she was close to seventy years old.

As soon as the conversation got really juicy, there was a certain adorable little girl with long pigtails and a sparkle in her eyes, who came hopping in on one foot. She was pretty confident in this ability. It was my five year old daughter, Dominique. By the way, I knew she had her own agenda today. She gave her grandmother a great big hug and told her she was very glad to see her. I knew Dominique was buttering up her grandmother for something. She knew how to add a lot of butter to that toast too (Smile). Dominique told her grandmother she could stay with us forever. My mother and I locked eyes and we both laughed at that comment. My mother said she would love to stay but who was going to look after grandpa? Our little darling thought about it for a second and said, grandpa can come and stay here forever too and daddy won't mind either. My mother and I connected eyes again and laughed even harder. Dominique knew she had our attention. She was up to bat. All bases were loaded and she was ready to knock the ball out of the park. I was thinking, here it comes. I did not know exactly what she wanted at the time but I knew it had to be good one. Can we go to the ice cream shop and play checkers? Grandma can go too, Dominique said. I just had a lot of things to do. Maybe later, I said. Momma, not later, this persistent little girl said. Why can't we go now? Now is a good time, right?

By this time, I felt I was caught dead in the middle. My mother (Ms. Really Old School) was giving me the stare down with the question written across her forehead saying, Who is going to win this battle? For starters, I thought, why can't my daughter see I have laundry to do and other chores later? Clean clothes are important, right? It had to get done now, right? It was Saturday. It was laundry day. I thought, let me not forsake the routine. If I get the laundry done in my allotted time, I could move on to the next chore on my list.

Fun right? Ugh! Of course not, but duty called. This is what I had to do to stay the course. I thought, stay the course, Rochelle. You can do this. No breaks, but I had stares from both directions. For a fleeting moment, I thought maybe I could ask my mom what I should do. No way--not in front of my daughter! How could I ask mom's opinion; she was from the generation where a clean house, clean clothes and great food were important every second of the day? It was too important. If I stopped now, the "laundry angels" would come get me (Smile).

I looked at my mother again, I looked at the laundry, and then I looked at my daughter. By this time, the washer had stopped. Perfect timing, I thought. I unloaded the washer and put that load in the dryer. I headed to pick up another load to put in the washer; then I stopped immediately and asked myself, what are you doing? So, I spun around and pointed to my mom and told her, Grab your purse and I will get my car keys. We are going to the ice cream shop to eat ice cream and play checkers. My mom's mouth could have dropped to the floor. My daughter was saying, yippee, in the background and hopping on one foot as usual. My daughter grabbed her grandmother's hand and said, You will have lots of fun with us and I will show you how to play checkers, Grandma, because I am really good at it. My mother was really speechless (that was a first).

The three of us had the greatest time in the small ice cream shop--laughing, eating and playing checkers. We were having dessert before dinner. This was unheard of with my mother but not with Grammie. Priceless again! I still remember this like it was yesterday.

Later that evening, my mother told me she did not know if she would have stopped in the middle or even had the courage to stop such an ingrained routine before everything was completed, but she understood. Additionally, she said I was a great mom and she was very proud of me for stopping and taking the time. She said I knew how to take advantage of the time. I did not wait for later.

It has been many years since but it is still relevant today--to take the time to be present. There is no time like now. My daughter, who is a young adult now, still remembers that time and mentions her memories of eating ice cream in the little shop and playing checkers. To tell the truth, I do not remember Dominique ever giving me credit for keeping the laundry done, or neatly folding it. On the other hand, I remember her telling me about the fun times we shared together. I am grateful. We are still creating memories.

Remember: **Joy is in the Now Place.**

What Can I Apply to My Life From This Chapter?

Until Next Time

I appreciate the time you have taken to invest in your life. I certainly hope that my book, "Joy is in the Now Place," has provided a framework for more joy in your life. I hope you were able to marinate on every single moment--to stop and be present during this process. My intention for writing this book was to share my life's journey, focusing on precious moments that made an impact on my life, and to inspire others along the way. There is much more value and joy to have when you take the time to experience, discover and examine your life. Do not wait until you are given permission. Give it to yourself. As I see it, you will gain even more joy and freedom when you are intentional. Do not rush through your life. Minimize living overwhelmed and frantic. Your life should not be dictated by what is going on outside of you, but predicated on the joy that is already inside of you. Concentrate on your life now. There is joy, power and purpose when you allow yourself to be present. Tap into it! Embrace it! Everyone benefits when you do. Serve well! Live Well!

Much peace always,

Rochelle
"Joy is in the Now Place"

Sources

American Journal of Clinical Nutrition. "*Looked at How Attention and Memory Affect Food Intake.*" April 2013. <*http://www.health.harvard.edu/blog/distracted-eating-may-add-to-weight-gain-201303296037*>

American Psychiatric Association. "*The Meaning, Process and the Positive Effects of Forgiveness.*" Compiled 2006 at the 59th Annual DPI/NGO Conference United Nations Headquarters Midday Workshop on Forgiveness. *https://www.apa.org/international/resources/publications/forgiveness.pdf*

Brandt, Andrea, PhD, M.F.T. *"How Do You Forgive When It Feels Impossible?"* Psychology Today Magazine. Sept 2014. <*https://www.psychologytoday.com/blog/mindful-anger/201409/how-do-you-forgive-even-when-it-feels-impossible*>

LeWine, Howard, MD. *"Distracted Eating May Add to Weight Gain,"* Harvard Health Publications-Harvard Medical School. March 2013. *http://www.health.harvard.edu/blog/distracted-eating-may-add-to-weight-gain-201303296037*

Mayo Clinic Staff. *"Stress Relief from Laughter? It's No Joke."*
Healthy Lifestyle Stress Management. *July 2013.*
<http://www.mayoclinic.org/healthy-lifestyle/stressmanagement/in-depth/stress-relief/art-20044456>

Sweet, Rose. *"Forgiveness and Restoration."*
Focus on The Family. 2001.
http://www.focusonthe family.com/marriage/divorce-and-infidelity/forgiveness-and-restoration/forgiveness-what-it-is-and-what-it-isnt#

Disclaimer

It is the sole responsibility of the reader and purchaser to adhere to all laws, regulations, jurisdictions, licensing, business practices and advertising in the United States and abroad.

Biography

Rochelle R. Asberry is the proud owner of Dominique's Enterprise LLC, a health and wellness company in Indianapolis, Indiana. She is a sought after Inspirational Public Speaker with a "No Excuse Approach," Author, Educator and Health Advocate for over 20 years. She has conducted and spoken at many conferences, organizations, Fortune 500 corporations, seminars and forums. Rochelle has been on television and in several newspapers and magazines as well. One of her strongest desires is to help people do well. She has a definite love and passion for people. Whether she is working with an individual, group or corporation, she has a definite voice for change. She is known for her natural ability of gaining audience attention and guiding people to their optimal potential.

In addition to all of her accomplishments, Rochelle is most proud of being a devoted wife and mom. Rochelle is an active member of her church for 20+ years where she serves in a leadership capacity and participates in many community efforts.

In her spare time, she loves to travel with her family, read, meet new people and experience different cuisines. Rochelle loves to have a great time and people enjoy being around her.